Everybody's Everywhere Backyard Bird Book

by the editors of Klutz Press

KLUTZ®

Development:
Sandra Craig, DeWitt Durham, Elaine Brett
Design and art direction: MaryEllen Podgorski
Cartoons: Ed Taber
Biological illustrations: Judy Waller
Photo research: Marta Kongsle
Photo credits appear on page 86.
Production: Jill S. Turney, Teshin Associates

Published by Klutz
Manufactured in Korea.
Birdcall manufactured
in the U.S.A.

ISBN 1-878257-26-9

Write Us

Klutz is an independent publisher located in Palo Alto, California, and staffed entirely by real human beings. We would love to hear your comments regarding this or any of our books.

KLUTZ®
2121 Staunton Court / Palo Alto, CA 94306

Additional Copies

For the location of your nearest Klutz retailer, call (415) 857-0888. If they should be tragically out of stock, additional copies of this book, as well as the entire library of "100% Klutz certified" books are available in our mail order catalogue. See back page.

4 1 5 8

How to Use the Audubon Birdcall

Roger Eddy, who manufactures the Audubon Birdcall for us, first encountered friction birdcalls in Italy, shortly after World War II, when he saw hunters using them to attract songbirds. In the years since, Roger has made and sold millions of them, always keeping a fanatical eye on quality.

The wooden part of the birdcall is birch, and the metal piece is pewter. By twisting the two parts together in slightly different ways, it is possible to make a variety of sounds. Holding the wooden part still while twisting the metal creates a different sound from the reverse. Try a few techniques, and you'll soon discover your birdcall is an instrument with many voices.

Table of Contents

INTRODUCTION

This is a bird guidebook for regular, non-bird people who, very much like yourself, know that birds have feathers, fly, and lay eggs in nests. That's all we require; we'll take you from there. The birds you will find in this guide are the kinds that are already all around you—flying outside your window, perched on your telephone wire, possibly even decorating your car.

Our first goal in writing this guide is simple: to enable you to put names to a flock of feathered strangers that have been flying around your life all these years. Turning strangers into friends is a sound lifelong practice—whether they swim, crawl, walk, or fly.

We've provided only a modest collection of the most common, all-over-the-continent birds. Obviously many birds of the less common sort haven't been covered. Once you've begun to take notice of the birds in your world (and you will soon be struck by the numbers once you start to recognize them) you will find yourself—perhaps even unwillingly—curious about them.

Shortly after that, you may find that our little guidebook doesn't take you far enough. And at that point we'll have achieved our second goal, the sneakier one, because then you will find yourself looking for more detailed information (see the Resources) and shortly after that you will lose the right to call yourself a "regular, non-bird person."

How We Organized the Bird Descriptions

By habitat. The first, most important question in bird identification is "Where am I?" So we broke down the possibilities into four categories:

 Cities

 Back yards, parks, small woods, and suburbia in general

 Open country and farmlands

 Around water

When you spot a mystery bird, look around you and flip to the appropriate section.

How to Identify Birds

A Step-by-Step Guide

Let's say you've spotted a bird and want to identify it. First, you consider the usual suspects for your area: robin, sparrow, pigeon, crow or whatever. Nothing that obvious? OK, that leaves you with a mystery bird. Time to assemble the clues. Ask yourself six pertinent questions.

1. ***Where are you?*** Mowing your lawn? Rappelling off a cliff? Wading at the beach? Playing catch at the park? On a city street?

2. ***Where's the bird?*** In a shrub? Treetop? On a wire? On the ground? By the water? Flying low? Flying high?

3. ***What's it doing?*** Hammering on a tree? Pulling out a worm? Perching on a branch? Screeching? Singing? Swooping? Soaring?

4. ***How big is it?*** Is it sparrow-sized? Pigeon-sized? Robin-sized? Crow-sized?

5. ***What is its shape?*** Stocky, slim, short-legged, long-legged? Is its tail forked? Square? Rounded? Pointed? Is its beak thick or thin? Long or short? Does it have a crest? What about its wings? Are they short, rounded, long, pointed?

6. ***Last, what are its color and markings?*** Does it have notable stripes or bars?

You can remember these six questions most easily by repeating the following immortal phrase: **Where, where, what big shape you color!**

This does not make particularly good sense. But repeat it to yourself anyway three times. See if it doesn't stick.

By answering these six questions and checking your answers against the information in the individual descriptions, you can generally narrow your suspects down pretty quickly.

A few of our birds can be recognized by their distinctive voices, but in general we have not emphasized bird sounds. If you can't tell the difference between *rikki rikki rikki* and *bzeet bzeet bzeet*, that's fine. You don't need to.

One final note: Although many birds will just be there—available for instant viewing with no effort at stealth on your part—you will see even more by sitting down in some likely habitat and just relaxing. No talking, and no movement. In addition, by using your birdcall, you will draw curious or feisty birds come to do battle with you for their territory.

Bird Words

crown
eyebrow
bill
tail
nape
back
shoulder
wing
bar
rump
chin
throat
wing
breast
belly
foot

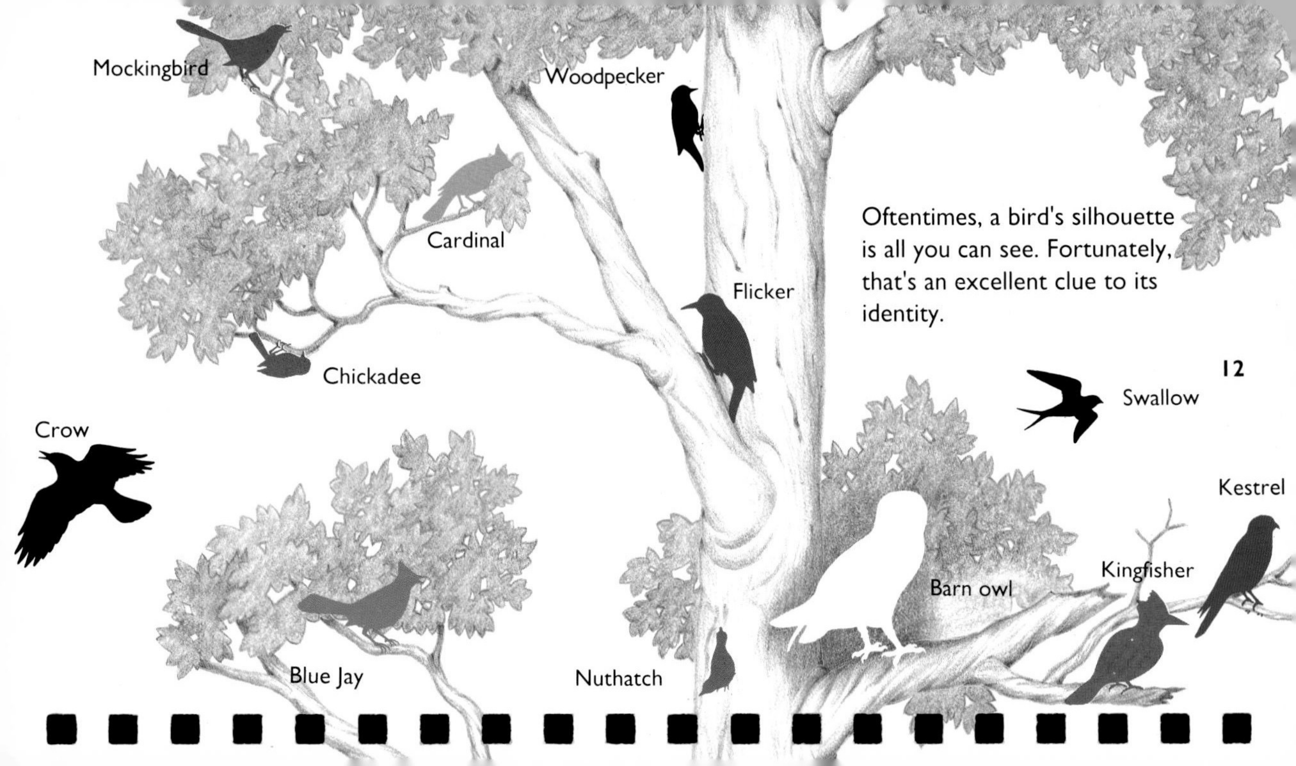

Oftentimes, a bird's silhouette is all you can see. Fortunately, that's an excellent clue to its identity.

Hummingbird
Meadowlark
Bluebird
Goldfinch
Great Blue Heron
Red-Winged Blackbird
Robin
Sparrow
Finch
Killdeer

Baby robins fresh out of the eggs.

What to Do If You Find a Baby Bird

If you find a baby bird so young it has no feathers, try to find the nest (it can't be far), then pick the baby up and replace it. Contrary to myth, it will not be abandoned simply because you touched it.

If your baby has feathers, it probably isn't abandoned. You may have to move it to a cat-safe spot, but then just leave it there and check on it. If its parents don't show up in an hour or so, take it inside and make a nest out of torn paper towels. Keep the baby warm with a light bulb or heating pad (warm, not hot) and call a local veterinarian or wildlife rescue group right away.

Attracting Birds to Your Yard

It's not hard to make your back yard a favorite among the local bird population if you provide it with water (preferably moving), food, and shelter from predators (i.e. cats).

Naturally, a well-placed bird feeder, especially if you have cold winters, will also bring in the birds. Fill it with birdseed from a pet shop; serve with a side order of bacon drippings when you get the chance. As always, locate food where cats can't climb to it and use a baffle or something to keep the squirrels at bay.

Birdhouses will attract certain species (like bluebirds, chickadees, house finches, starlings, and a few others), but trees and shrubs and an uncut lawn will attract an even larger group. If your trees or shrubs are fruit-bearing, then you've provided room and board in one easy stop.

Why Do Birds Do What They Do?

Once you start to look closely, you will see birds doing a million different things—many of which will make no sense to a human observer like yourself. But even though the connection may be far from obvious, a great deal of bird behavior falls into two huge categories: finding food and finding a mate.

A third category, a little smaller, consists of things birds do to prevent becoming food themselves. Of course, birds use a myriad of different strategies for accomplishing these goals, hence the huge differences that exist among

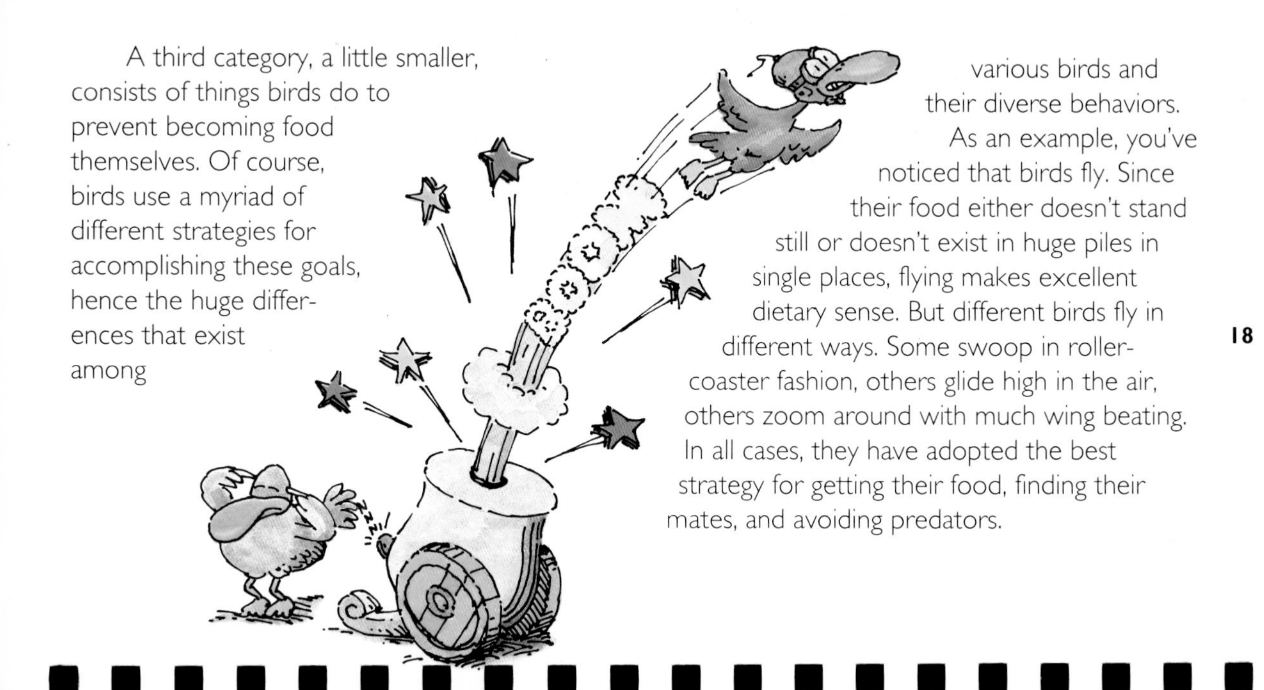

various birds and their diverse behaviors. As an example, you've noticed that birds fly. Since their food either doesn't stand still or doesn't exist in huge piles in single places, flying makes excellent dietary sense. But different birds fly in different ways. Some swoop in roller-coaster fashion, others glide high in the air, others zoom around with much wing beating. In all cases, they have adopted the best strategy for getting their food, finding their mates, and avoiding predators.

Some birds spend a great deal of time in the water, some on tree trunks. Again, this is not whimsical. They have adapted to their environment, and they're coping with its requirements and achieving their goals as best they can.

Having said that, it should also be noted that every rule has its exceptions. Even bird experts are baffled by a few, particularly peculiar bird behaviors. You are invited to explain why chickens, to take one example, love to take "dust baths." (A chicken will often pick up a beakful of dust, toss it into the air, and revel in the dirty mess that follows.)

Or you might try to explain why some birds have a thing about ants—not eating them but "bathing" in them. A few bird types will squat over anthills, letting ants run all over them. Others will pick up one ant at a time and place it carefully under a wing.

A kingfisher picks up dinner with a sudden plunge.

The Right Part for the Right Job

Physically, birds have bodies that "make sense" when you see what they do. Seed crackers have short, stout beaks. Trunk climbers have two toes facing forward and two toes facing backward. Gliders have big wings. Meat eaters have sharp claws, or talons. Water dippers or flower suckers have long, probing bills. Swimmers have webbed toes. By looking at these body clues, you can often make a pretty good guess as to what sorts of food a bird eats, and how the bird gets around.

A hummingbird's beak

A flicker's foot

An owl's talon

A flicker's tongue

A cardinal's beak

A duck's foot

Where Do Birds Live? And When Do They Live There?

Nearly every sort of bird has favorite kinds of places where you can typically find it. They might be wooded areas, lawns, roadsides, tall grassy fields, treetops, shrubs, riverbanks, wherever. Sometimes, when it's hard to say just by appearance, you can identify a bird simply by the place you see it. Keep that in mind when you read the descriptions that follow. They all include where-you-usually-see-them information, and that can be a useful clue in close call situations.

Incidentally, the reason birds have favorite haunts is usually nutritional. They hang out where their food lives. Woodpeckers don't hop around on lawns because they can't get to the earthworms underground. And robins don't poke around on poles because they can't get to the grubs in them.

Finding a ready meal is also a large part of the reason many birds head south for the winter. But, contrary to what you might guess, not all birds migrate. A good number are real locals —they don't ever move. Those that choose to stick it out in snow country have figured out ways to make do. (If you want to be a real bird-pal, set out a feeder with seed at first snowfall.)

Spring and fall are traveling times for the migrators, and your chance of seeing something unusual for your area is best during these two seasons. You're likely to see more birds in the mornings and evenings, when the bugs are out. A few exceptions (owls, for example) are noted in the descriptions.

How Do Birds Steer When They Migrate?

It's a bit of a mystery. Migrating birds are capable of astonishingly accurate navigation, and they appear to use a number of overlapping systems to do it. They look for landmarks and smell the local smells. They sense wind direction, sun and star position, and, most mysteriously, on cloudy days they sense the earth's magnetic field. But the details of how they put all this together, or which systems they rely on the most, are still debated.

In North America, there are four well-defined north-south "flyways" by which migratory birds travel when the seasons dictate. Flyways are bird highways, and during the spring and fall migration seasons, serious bird watchers may be found encamped along them, looking for rare birds passing through on their way to winter or summer homes.

What Kind of Parents Are Birds?

It varies a good deal. Some baby birds (called "hatchlings") are born naked and helpless and need a great deal of care for quite a while. Others are born with downy feathers and better developed muscles and are generally much more ready for the world.

Parenting styles are appropriately attentive in each case.

Incidentally, the inside of a hatchling's mouth is often a bright color, the better to attract attention when it is held wide open in the "Feed me, I'm yours" mode.

How a Chick Hatches

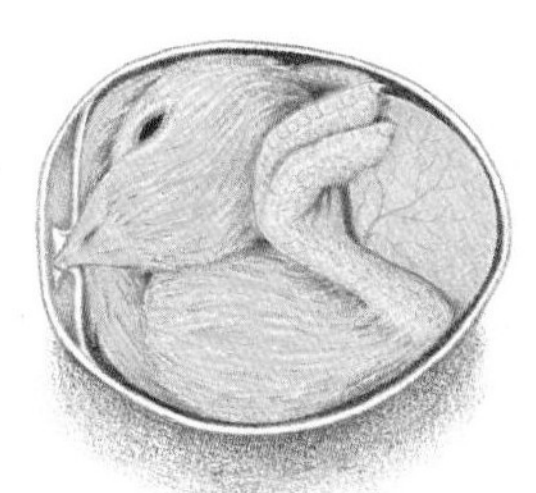

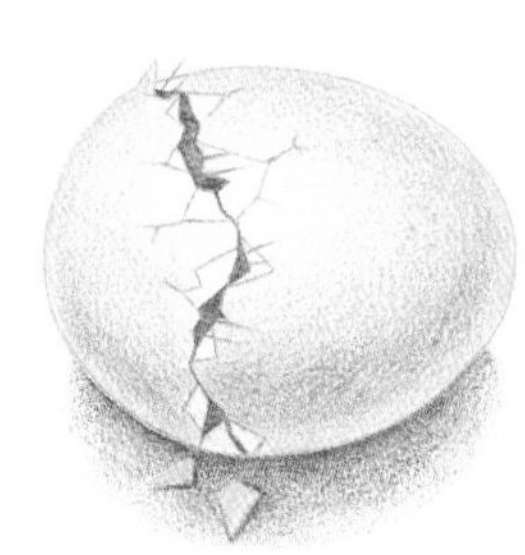

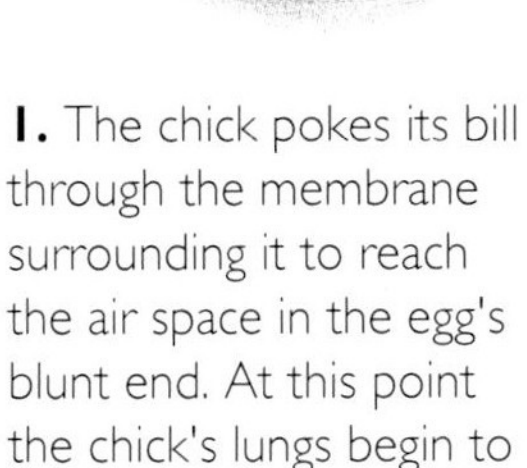

1. The chick pokes its bill through the membrane surrounding it to reach the air space in the egg's blunt end. At this point the chick's lungs begin to work.

2. The chick breaks a small hole in the eggshell—a process called pipping—which admits more air and fosters lung development.

3. After a delay of 15 to 40 hours, the chick hammers a circle of small holes in the top of the shell.

4. The chick presses down with its feet and pushes its shoulders up, forcing the top of the shell off.

Do Birds Get Married for Life?

Most of them don't, although swans, geese, eagles, some owls, and a few others do. The rest of them pair up for a few seasons at most. During the courtship phase, when the males are looking for a new mate, they engage in all sorts of elaborate "look-at-me" kinds of behavior. After mating, it's the male that usually brings food to the female rather than vice versa (as in some other species one could name).

Nest building often takes place during the courtship period, and the nests are as varied as the kinds of birds that build them. Some birds do nothing but scrape shallow depressions in the ground (killdeers), others get by with existing holes or cavities (owls, bluebirds), and still others make nests out of mud (swallows). Some nests are messy and careless (pigeons'), while others are tightly woven, proud homes (goldfinches').

Orioles are quality homemakers. Their nests are neatly woven and hang from supporting branches.

A few days after mating, the eggs are laid. How many depends on the type of bird and the fatness of the land. Scarce food means fewer eggs. The eggs have to be kept at an even temperature, and the task of sitting on them usually falls upon the female, although not in every case. Some species share the job quite fairly. It's a job, incidentally, that lasts anywhere from 12 days for small eggs (like those of the house finch) to 28 days for large eggs (the great blue heron's).

Why Do Birds Sing or Call?

Birds make noises for the same reason you do—to communicate: to tell someone where they are, to warn somebody else to scram, to attract a special somebody's attention, or to sound an alarm. When they are used to defend a territory or attract a mate, they are called "songs." Songs come from the males, and they are not instinctive so much as learned from other males. "Calls" are used to stay in touch with other birds, and they seem to be strictly instinct, known from birth.

Do Birds Sleep?

Most birds get busy when the sun rises and relax when it goes down. Like most animals in the food chain, they sleep watchfully. With birds, however, sleeping is called roosting, and they often do it in large groups, owing to the safety factor of a crowd.

You may have wondered, with good reason, why a bird perched on a limb doesn't fall off when it falls asleep. The reason is that the tendons in a bird's leg tighten up when it sleeps, its claws becoming tight fists around the branch.

How Well Do Birds See and Hear?

Because bird meals tend to be small, or fast-moving, or both, birds rely on their eyes quite heavily. When they are looking for detail, birds will use a single eye—a robin with a cocked head, for example, is looking with one eye for earthworms. When they need good depth perception, as a hawk does when zooming down on a sparrow, they use both eyes. It should come as no surprise, under these circumstances, to learn that the eyes of a robin are set far back in its head, facilitating single-eye looking, while those of a hawk are set far forward.

Birds of prey (hawks, eagles, kestrels) have better eyes than you, but many birds do not. They may see things better than you, but that's only because they look more closely.

Birds have excellent hearing, even though they have ear holes, not ear flaps. To give you an idea of how good, woodpeckers can hear the sound of grubs inside tree trunks, and owls hunt primarily by sound, being quite deadly even in pitch blackness.

Feathers and Molting

Birds dress in feathers for a number of sound, functional reasons. They are lightweight (a handy point if flying is how you get around). They're warm, they shed water, and, of course, they're very attractive. Ask any peacock. When feathers wear out, which they do all the time, they fall out and new ones grow in to replace them—a process called molting. In some birds, the kinds that spend a great deal of time in flight, that's a continuous process. Other birds, ducks particularly, molt all at once during certain times of the year. At those times, usually only a couple of weeks, the ducks cannot fly.

BIRD DESCRIPTIONS

Pigeon

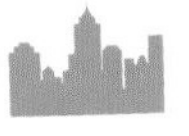

Pigeons have the unfortunate PR problem of survival success. Centuries ago, in Europe, they used to nest on rocky cliffs, where their numbers were largely kept in check by hawks and falcons. But for pigeons, times have changed for the better. Building ledges are far more common than rocky ledges, and hawks and falcons are in some decline. Add to those factors a hearty, non-judgmental appetite for just about anything organic, and you have a successful species adaptation. Pigeons (or **rock doves**, as they are officially called) have thrived in city environments to the point where they've been called "rats with feathers."

But it's an unfair rap. For one thing, pigeons have the distinction of being perhaps the oldest domesticated animal of them all. Alexander the Great, Julius Caesar, and Hannibal all used carrier pigeons to relay battlefront news. So did both sides of both modern world wars.

One carrier pigeon received a medal (the Purple Heart?) when it delivered its message despite having had a leg shot off.

Pigeons were originally brought from Europe by early settlers. Today, the raising and training of homing pigeons is more popular than ever. Stories of their speed and homing ability are legendary and often make it into the "believe it or not" columns. Homing pigeons can be blindfolded and transported across hundreds of miles of unfamiliar territory. When released, they will generally return at top speed in a direct, unwavering line. How? The sun plays a role, but at night, or on cloudy days, it appears that the pigeons are able to directly sense the earth's magnetic field lines.

A final footnote: Peregrine falcons, a seriously endangered species once found only in remote wilderness areas, have recently been introduced experimentally into the unwilderness environs of New York City, Los Angeles, and Boston. Breeding pairs have had some success, and it is now possible to see a peregrine falcon nest on the Empire State Building. As anticipated, the falcons prey on pigeons, utilizing their 150-mile-per-hour diving speed to much advantage.

Appearance: 13". Plump bird with small head. Typical birds are gray with iridescent neck feathers, white rump, two black wing bars, dark tail tip. Other colors have resulted from selective breeding, including all-black, all-white, piebald, and reddish brown. Sexes similar.

House Sparrow

Perhaps the most populous of all North American birds, the house sparrow lives in all 48 lower states. If you spot a small, gray, chirpy bird and can't really tell what it is, say "sparrow." You'll be right most of the time.

House sparrows are often brought up when the evils of introduced species are discussed. They are not native to North America but were brought over from Europe in the 1850s to control insect pests. At first, sparrows thrived on horse feed until the advent of cars tightened up that supply. However, like any good adaptor, they have since found many substitutes, and today they will turn up their beaks at very little that looks organic. In city parks they make bold little beggars, looking for handouts.

Some native species—for example, bluebirds and martins—have suffered as sparrows proliferated, but on the other side, house finches often out-compete sparrows for nesting sites and habitat. In cities, suburbs, and farmlands, sparrows build nests (large balls of grasses, weeds, and trash) into any cavity they can find.

Appearance: 6". Streaked brown above, gray below. **Male:** Gray crown, whitish cheeks, chestnut nape, black throat. **Female:** Brown crown, buffy eyebrows, plain breast.

Appearance: Baltimore oriole: 7–8".
Male: Bright orange and black with solid black head. **Female:** Olive-brown above, burnt orange-yellow below; two white wing bars.
Bullock's oriole (shown here): 7–8½".
Male: Distinguished from Baltimore by orange cheeks and eyebrow and white wing patches. **Female:** Grayer back and whiter belly than Baltimore.

Northern Oriole

The Baltimore oriole (the bird, not the baseball team) is otherwise known as the eastern oriole. Up until the mid-1980s, it was distinguished from the western (or Bullock's). But since both look enough alike, and interbreed freely anyway, the two species were recently, and officially, merged into the northern oriole.

The eastern brand is identified easily by its striking colors, which probably got it into the baseball mascot business in the first place: bright orange and black with a solid black head. The western male differs mostly in that it has orange cheeks and eyebrows and white wing patches.

The northern oriole lives commonly in the suburbs, city parks, and woods. During the winter, eucalyptus trees are a favorite hangout. Orioles will eat insects, fruit, and nectar. Orange slices in your bird feeder will often attract them.

Northern orioles are champion builders whose nests are architectural marvels: deep, hanging pouches of intricately woven plant fibers, hair, string, and Spanish moss (in the South) lined with wool, fine grass stems, and cottony materials. These elaborate, solid constructions can be most clearly seen in the leafless limbs of a winter tree.

Appearance: 3–3½". Very small bird with a long, slender, strawlike bill for reaching into flowers. Iridescent green above, whitish below. **Male:** Has brilliant red throat (which may appear black or dark in poor light), black tail with shallow fork. **Female:** Lacks the red, has black fan-shaped tail tipped with white spots.

Ruby-Throated Hummingbird

If you created a category of "Animals That Shouldn't Work," you might very well start the list with hummingbirds. Physically, they appear highly un-aerodynamic. Tiny wings, fat body. It looks like a back-to-the-drawing-board kind of design.

But, in fact, hummingbirds might be the most amazing fliers of all. Their wings move so fast they appear to be nothing but blurs. Hummers can stop, hover, back up, shoot forward... all in an instant. Their metabolism is so high (it has to be to keep those wings moving) that they eat constantly. Their diet is flower nectar, small insects, and spiders, and they are not shy about getting it. They will challenge bumblebees for flowers and zoom up to inspect people wearing bright, flowered clothing.

Hummingbirds exist throughout North America, but the ruby-throated variety lives only in the East. It lives in woods, gardens, and parks and co-exists well with people. Its nest, made of plant down and fibers, can be found attached to small branches. The walls are usually quite thick, leaving only a tiny cavity inside for a hummer's equally tiny eggs.

A hummingbird's nest would fit easily in the palm of your hand.

Appearance:
9–11". Gray above, lighter below; large white patches on wings. Slimmer, longer-tailed than a robin. Yellow eyes.

Northern Mockingbird

If meadowlarks are the classical musicians of the fields, mockingbirds are the pop stars of the suburbs. They can compose their own songs, borrow from other species, imitate barking dogs, sirens, a beeper on a dump truck—you name it. During moonlit summer nights they can sing all night long, defending their territory against the world while keeping an entire neighborhood awake.

You'll see them most easily perched in the tops of trees. They're fiercely territorial birds and like to keep a sharp eye out for interlopers. If you place a feeder in a mockingbird's territory, even if it contains food that a mockingbird wouldn't touch, the mockingbird will post a stakeout and run off any trespassers.

Mockingbirds seem fairly tolerant of people and all of our constructions. They live in cities, suburbs, farmlands, woods, and along open roads. Their nests are built in trees or shrubs, and they contain twigs, dry leaves, moss, and small roots.

Appearance: 7½ – 9". Crested, with the heavy, strong, conical bill of the seed-eater, in this case reddish.
Male: Bright red with black face.
Female: Buffy brown with some red on crest, wings, and tail.

Northern Cardinal

It's hard to keep a low profile when you're always dressed in cardinal red, and the northern cardinal proves it. One of the top five on our unofficial list of "Birds Even You Used to Be Able to Identify," the cardinal is our third major league baseball bird (see blue jays and orioles for the other two).

Cardinals mate for life, unlike most birds, and live in apparent harmony all year. As proof, they will often complete each other's sentences: one bird (the male?) will begin the phrase and the other (the you-know-who) will trill out the musical conclusion.

During courtship, the male will bring morsels of food to the female, and after a brood is born, he will continue to feed them after the female starts preparing for another lot.

Cardinals eat berries, fruit, seeds, and insects, and they love bird feeders, which have probably been responsible for the cardinal's increased range and numbers. Their nests are loosely built of twigs, vines, grasses, and weed stalks, and are lined with hair and fine grass stalks. Nests are usually placed in dense shrubbery or among tangled vines.

The northern cardinal can be found nearly anywhere there are trees and grass: suburban yards, gardens, fringes of woods, thickets, and parks.

Appearance: 11–12". Crested, bright blue above, light gray below, black necklace and eye stripe, white spots and black bars on wings and tail. Sexes alike.

Steller's jay

Scrub jay

Blue Jay

The original party animals, blue jays are loud, aggressive, and generally disruptive. A single blue jay, with a rush of wings and a banzai cry, will scatter a group of songbirds at a feeder and help him or herself to everything available. If a cat is nearby, a jay will frequently divebomb it, pulling up at the last instant to perch in a nearby branch and emit its hard-to-ignore screech. Another questionable blue jay habit is to raid the nests of smaller birds, stealing eggs or young chicks.

In their defense, though, it should be noted that jays play an important (but unconscious) role in replanting forests because of their habit of burying acorns. Besides acorns, blue jays like to hide all sorts of food (nuts, seeds, fruit, insects, baby birds, and eggs). In the same slightly paranoid vein, jays become uncharacteristically quiet and reclusive around their nests, which they tend to hide away in dense tree foliage.

The blue jay is only found east of the Rockies, but its western relatives are the Steller's jay, and the similar scrub jay. The Steller's has the easily recognized blue jay crest; the scrub does not. Besides their screech, blue jays are also capable of a musical *queedle, queedle*, and, like true cut-ups, can mimic the sound of other birds.

House Finch

Another member of the small, hard-to-tell-the-difference-between-them family of small chirpy birds (unofficially known as SCBs). House finches originally came from the West, but they were illegally transported to New York in the 1940s (when they had some West Coast cachet and were known glamorously as "Hollywood Finches"). Their territory is now expanded and includes both coasts and parts of the Midwest.

Finches have a similar appearance to sparrows, the lead member of the SCB family. Since the two compete for the same food and nest sites, the sparrow population often suffers when finches invade the same territory. Within their range, they live nearly everywhere: cities, suburbs, parks, farmlands, desert scrub, canyons. They eat typical bird fare—seeds, insects, berries. Their nest is built of grass, leaves, and twigs, and they build in shrubs and trees.

Their call is a single chirp, but males can also sing out in a varied warble that sounds like a canary. When they fly in groups, which is often, they are known colorfully as a "charm of finches."

Appearance: 5–5¾". Similar to sparrows, with streaky brown back, wings, and belly. **Male:** Red forehead, eyebrow, breast, and rump. **Female:** Lacks the red, has brown head.

Appearance:
4¾ – 5¾".
Black cap and throat, white cheek patches, gray back, lighter below, buffy sides. Sexes similar.

Black-Capped Chickadee

These are small, plump, high-energy birds who pop from branch to branch looking around with much goodwill and curiosity. Their black cap is the easiest way to distinguish them from other small birds. After raising their young (midsummer), they form small flocks that roost and search for food together through the winter. When one of them finds a tidbit, the others quickly join in. And when another spots a predator, the flock will freeze and take up the cry collectively.

The chickadee eats insects, seeds, and berries, and during the winter it will be happy to stop by your feeder if you keep suet or sunflower seeds in it. Chickadees nest in holes that they make in rotten trees or stumps, or they'll move into natural cavities or abandoned woodpecker holes. They live in wooded areas of almost any kind.

Chickadee's popsicle stop.

Appearance: 5–6". Small, stubby bird with short tail, short legs, and strong feet; long, strong bill similar to a woodpecker's. Blue-gray above, black crown and nape, black eyes in white face, white below, chestnut under tail. Female similar but with dark gray crown and nape.

White-Breasted Nuthatch

Nuthatch has a nice appropriate ring to it when you're talking about the only bird in America that insists on walking *down* a tree trunk rather than up it. Why exactly the nuthatch looks for his grubs and insects this particular way is up for discussion. One theory: The upside-down view lets them see bugs that woodpeckers miss (both the white-breasted nuthatch and the downy woodpecker occupy the same territory and eat the same diet).

The nuthatch has unusually long toes and long, down-turned claws that enable it to do its anti-gravity acrobatics (the nuthatch is just as happy hanging down from a branch, batlike, as perched on top of the branch).

The nuthatch's bill, like that of a woodpecker, is long and pointy—good for reaching into crevices for bugs. (Other than insects, nuthatches will eat seeds and, at a feeder, suet and bacon drippings.)

You can see nuthatches most anywhere there are trees: parks, woods, suburbs, roadsides. They nest in natural tree holes or, if the chance presents itself, they'll claim an abandoned woodpecker hole.

Appearance: 12–14". Brown back with dark bars, buff with black spots below, black patch on upper breast. **Yellow-shafted**: yellow under wings and tail; black mustache and red on nape (male only). **Red-shafted**: red under wings and tail; male has red mustache. **Gilded**: yellow wing and tail linings, red mustache.

Northern Flicker

The northern flicker is a woodpecker, along with the downy, the only other one in this collection. Like all woodpecker varieties, the flicker will drum away at trees and stumps, but it is the only one in North America who will forage on the ground as well, searching for fruit, seeds, insects, and especially ants. The northern flicker, a serious consumer of ants, has a perfect ant-eater tongue: long and sticky.

In appearance, the northern flicker varies from territory to territory. It always has a brown back with dark bars, while underneath it is buff with black spots, but in the East it has yellow patches under wings and tail, and the male has a black mustache. In the West, the patches and mustache are red. In the southwestern deserts, it has a red mustache (the male) but yellow wing and tail linings.

The flicker lives in woodlands, farmlands, suburbs, and deserts, and it nests in holes dug into trees, telephone poles, fence posts, or, in the desert, large cacti. You can identify flickers and other woodpeckers on the wing by their wavy flight. On tree trunks flickers and woodpeckers move up in short hops, bracing themselves with their stiff tails.

A gilded flicker snug in its cactus home.

Downy Woodpecker

You'll probably hear a downy woodpecker before you see it. A high-speed drumming from somewhere up a tree trunk or telephone pole will be the giveaway.

The downy woodpecker is a territorial bird. It likes to stake out an area all its own. The loud hammering you often hear is its way of telling neighboring birds where its turf is. When it pecks at a tree trunk for food (grubs or insects of almost any kind), the sound is much quieter and less drumlike.

After pecking out a hole, the downy has a long, sticky tongue for those hard-to-reach bugs. Its brain, in case you were wondering, is insulated from all the jarring.

The downy woodpecker lives commonly in parks, suburbs, forests, and orchards. It eats—in addition to any bugs it can find inside trees and telephone poles—many seeds and berries. (As a result, it is a frequent visitor to bird feeders.) Its nest is a small, circular hole pecked out of a dead tree or fencepost.

Appearance: 6½". The smallest woodpecker in North America. Small, slender, chisel-shaped bill; strong feet with two toes forward and two back; black and white above, white below; black and white striped cheeks; male has small red patch on nape.

Appearance: 9–11". **Male:** Dark gray above with blackish head and tail, brick-red or orange breast, white throat with dark stripes. **Female:** Similar but duller.

American Robin

Perhaps the only bird you can already name. The robin redbreast (actually, it's a little more orange than red, truth to tell) is the legendary "harbinger of spring." It's such a well-known bird, celebrated on stage and screen, that many people have unconsciously made it into "Everybird." As a result, these people think that all birds eat worms and stalk across the lawn with that peculiar stop-and-start gait.

They don't actually, but it's a tribute to the robin's popularity that the mistake is made.

The robin has especially good vision and a keen eye for small movements near at hand, the kind that worms make. When it spots one, the stabbing motion is almost too quick to follow.

As you might have suspected, the robin lives nearly anywhere it can find grassy areas to hunt in: cities, suburbs, fields, parks, gardens. Besides worms, robins will also partake of insects and (especially in the winter) berries. In the late winter, after having had a few too many fermented berries, robins have been known to get drunk enough to fly into windows and pass out.

Its nest is a deep cup made of grasses, weed stalks, and mud, usually built in shrubs or tree forks, or on building ledges. Its eggs, by the way, are usually three or four in number and robin's-egg blue in color.

Appearance: 9–11", the size of a robin. Thin, black bill. Brown above, white below; two black bands on breast; rufous rump and tail.

Killdeer

An ideal bird for the birder with no head for names. The killdeer's call is a shrill, clear, helpful "*kill-deer, kill-deer.*" The killdeer nests on the ground and relies on an unusual strategy to protect its nest. When an intruder comes too close, it will leap into the air with a sudden cry and flap around theatrically, dragging a "lame" wing and leading the predator far from the nest. After a few more Academy-Award-winning moments, the killdeer will miraculously recover and fly away.

Since the nest is on the ground, the killdeer and its nestlings depend on camouflage for protection. Their coloring blends imperceptibly into rocky, mixed-color backgrounds. They live in open spaces, away from streets and houses—pastures, parks, golf courses, woods, and mudflats, for instance—and they eat insects and seeds.

Appearance: 9". A chunky bird, streaked brown and buff above, striped head, yellow breast with black V, short tail with white outer feathers displayed in flight. Western meadowlark paler above, has more yellow on face. Sexes identical.

Meadowlark

The greatest voice in the wilds. Meadowlarks are justly famous for their song which, at least for the western variety, sounds like a ten-note phrase from a flute. The eastern variety (which looks much like the western, but sounds quite different) sings two clear slurred whistles, musical and pulled out: *tee-yah, tee-yair.*

Like most birds, the meadowlark sings to communicate, either to attract potential mates or to warn off potential competitors.

The meadowlark, unlike many of the people-tolerant birds in this book, can only really thrive in open farmland, fields, prairies, meadows, pastures, and the like. Shopping centers and housing developments do not agree with it, so it is suffering from a loss of habitat.

You'll see the meadowlark most often close to the ground or perched on a fencepost. At mealtimes it looks for insects and seeds. Its nest is on the ground, covered with a dome-shaped canopy of grasses woven into surrounding vegetation. The opening is on the side, and the eggs, if you're lucky enough to peek inside, are usually smooth, white, and splotched with brown and lavender.

American Goldfinch

The goldfinch is a bird that definitely likes the company of its own kind. You're much more likely to see a flock of them, startled out of a field, than a single goldfinch off by its lonesome. It's a tiny yellow bird that is almost always found near thistle plants, with which it has a close, dependent relationship. Not only does it feed its nestlings largely on thistle seeds, but it also uses thistledown to line its nest.

The goldfinch lives in almost any open woods or fields where it can find a patch of weeds and thistles. Its nest is craftily woven and lined; a small, neat double cup that has to be protected from the rain lest it fill up and drown the nestlings. Its diet is almost entirely small seeds—thistle and dandelion especially—and it flies in an energetic, roller-coaster style.

Appearance: 5". Short, conical, seed-cracking bill. **Summer, male:** Bright yellow with black forehead, tail, and wings with white wingbars. **Summer, female:** Dull yellow-olive, darker above, with black wings with white wingbars. **Winter:** Both sexes like the summer female but more gray-brown with yellow on throat.

Eastern Bluebird

Beautiful eastern bluebirds were once as common as robins, but in this century their number has decreased drastically. Bluebirds nest in cavities, as do house sparrows and starlings, which were introduced from Europe. The aggressive sparrows and starlings flourished and grabbed more and more of the available nest cavities. Meanwhile, dead trees were being cut down, and wood fenceposts were being replaced with metal ones, further reducing nest sites. Bluebirds were in danger of disappearing completely until people began building birdhouses to accommodate them. Entire "bluebird trails"—strings of birdhouses along country roads—have been established in parts of the country, and eastern bluebirds are making a comeback.

In the Rocky Mountain states and westward, the similar western bluebird replaces its eastern cousin, and the mountain bluebird can also be found in western mountains.

Appearance: 7". A little larger than a sparrow; has large dark eyes and a slender bill; often sits in a hunched posture. **Male:** Bright blue head, nape, back, wings, and tail; rusty throat and breast; white belly. **Female:** Similar to male but duller; head, nape, and back tinged with brown. The male **western** bluebird has a rusty patch on his blue back; the **mountain** bluebird is all sky blue, with no rust. Again, the females are paler.

Appearance: 6–7¾". Slim, sparrow-sized bird with deeply forked ("swallow") tail, long pointed wings, short bill, tiny feet; blue-black above, cinnamon-buff below (female is paler), with darker throat.

Barn Swallow

The barn swallow is an impressively agile flier, constantly jinking one way or another to catch flying insects in its open mouth. It's a feeding pattern and an athletic talent that makes it easy to recognize. If you spot a group of small birds with pointed slender wings, all of them zigging and zagging like crazy, chances are good you're looking at a descent of barn swallows.

You can see barn swallows most easily in the morning or evening (mealtimes). They're happy in all kinds of open areas, but they have a particular fondness for lakes and rivers (where the bugs are). They also seem to have no objection to living around people and buildings. Their nests are mud and straw cups, lined with feathers and plastered to beams, walls, eaves of barns, under bridges, and so on.

"Open wide." Adult swallows open wide to scoop insects mid-flight. These babies are in training.

American Crow

These days, if you spot a group of largish black birds, chances are you're looking a murder of crows ("murder" being an old-fashioned word for flock when you're talking about crows). If they begin to make a harsh "cawing" sound, that seals the case.

Crows are intelligent birds who like to travel in groups. Their ability to learn new behaviors in a changing environment is one of the reasons they're as common as they are. Bird trainers have been able to teach them to imitate human speech, and they tend to be quick learners for the kinds of problems that are put to them in "bird labs." If you "caw" at a crow, chances are very good he'll caw right back at you.

Crows are not picky eaters: insects, small reptiles, mice, eggs, small birds, clams, carrion, fruit crops (much to the farmers' dismay). They are also supposedly collectors of shiny objects, and they have a well-recorded lack of concern for scarecrows.

Crows live nearly everywhere and build big basket nests of sticks, bark, grass, fur, leaves, whatever. You'll often see the nests in the crotches of tree trunks.

Appearance: 17–21". A large chunky bird, completely black, with strong black bill and feet; forward-pointing bristles cover the nostrils. Sexes alike.

Appearance: 9–12". Small, robin-sized falcon with long, pointed wings, short, hooked bill, and large feet tipped with talons. **Male (shown here):** Rusty with black bars above, buff or white with black spots below, blue-gray wings. **Female (shown below):** rusty with black bars above, buff or white with rusty streaks below. Both have blue-gray and rust crown and white cheeks with two vertical black stripes.

American Kestrel

The kestrel (also known as the sparrow hawk, because of its size) seems like a smallish bird for a meateater. You might see it perched on a wire, or in a dead tree. You'll recognize it most easily, though, by the distinctive way it hunts—hovering on rapidly beating wings, 20 or 30 feet over open ground. If it spots a mouse, it will plunge in a sudden, efficient dive.

The kestrel lives nearly everywhere: along roadsides, in open country, farmlands, parks, suburbs, even cities. It nests in tree cavities or under the eaves of buildings.

Appearance: 14–20". A slender owl. Golden brown with gray mottling above, white below; white heart-shaped face, dark eyes; long, knock-kneed legs covered with bristly white feathers. Sexes identical.

Barn Owl

Because of its tolerance for humans, as well as its fondness for the rodents that have thrived around our farm buildings, the barn owl has become the most numerous owl in North America.

Barn owls are night animals and mouse-eating machines. Farmers welcome them into their barns. Their vision in poor light is excellent, but their hearing is nothing short of phenomenal. Across a pitch black barn, an owl can hear and locate a mouse. It's a feat that no radar set can duplicate and has been the subject of some research. The secret, apparently, has to do with the owl's accurate ability to sense which of its ears is receiving the sound first.

Of course no discussion of the owl is complete without mentioning its swivel-head act. Because its eyes are relatively fixed in their sockets, and because its radar-ears need to move around in order to zero in on mice locations, the owl's head has an amazing range of motion: it can turn 270° around, and almost entirely upside down.

The barn owl lives in open woodlands, grasslands, marshes, farms, even suburbs and cities. Besides mice, it will eat almost any small mammal up to the size of a jackrabbit. It nests in tree cavities, inside unused buildings, or in underground burrows. Its call, incidentally, is not a hoot but a long, rasping screech.

Appearance: 20–28". **Male:** Glossy green head, white neck ring, chestnut breast, gray body, white tail, blue wing patch, yellow bill, orange feet. **Female:** Mottled brown, blue wing patch, whitish tail, orange bill with black patch, orange feet.

Mallard

Although there are many different species of ducks, chances are most of the ducks you've seen in your life have been mallards. They're far and away the most common duck in North America and probably the world. They can nest on practically any body of water—a backyard wading pool, the town hall fountain, a wilderness pond—and will return faithfully to the same spot year after year.

Mallards are quite tolerant of people and will waddle up cheerfully for handouts. They have been domesticated for ages and are probably the ancestors of most breeds of domestic ducks. In China, mallards are particularly prized for their eggs, down, and meat.

Besides anything they can mooch from you, mallards eat grasses, seeds, water plants, insects, snails, and small fish. Their nests are built of cattails, reeds, and grasses and are lined with down. They're generally well hidden from foxes and other predators in tall grasses or dead reeds.

The mallard is a medium-sized duck, typically two feet in length when full grown. Most of the time males and females look very different, but for a few weeks in late summer, the male loses his distinctive coloring (it's described by birders as "going into eclipse"), and the only difference is in the color of their bills.

Incidentally, it's only the female that goes *quack quack*. The male utters a much less compelling *yeeb yeeb*.

Canada Goose

If it's possible to call a bird responsible, then the Canada goose has to qualify. Not only does it mate for life but it treats its parental obligations with a very un-birdlike degree of maturity. Goslings (baby geese) are watched long after they can fly and feed themselves, and when the family swims, mother and father take the front and rear while the kids arrange themselves in a neat line between them.

Canada geese are the most common kind of geese you will see. They are far more tolerant of people than their more reclusive and less numerous relatives. They like fresh or saltwater ponds, but can also be found near rivers or by marshes, grainfields, and grasslands. Your chances of seeing them are probably best when they travel. They fly quite high in noisy, V-shaped convoys—tightly arranged when migrating south, loosely organized when just moving around to a new feeding ground.

Canada geese eat grasses, seeds, grain, aquatic plants, and small animals. Their nest is a mound of sticks, cattails, reeds, and grasses often built on a low stump or mound near the water.

Appearance: 25–34"; great variation in size from short-necked, mallard-sized birds to long-necked, almost swan-sized birds. Black head and neck with white chin strap, gray-brown body, white under tail; black bill and legs. Sexes alike.

Appearance:

42–52"; may stand 4 feet tall; a very large, long-legged bird. Medium gray with narrow plumes over back and breast, white head with two black crown stripes extending into narrow black plumes from nape, black and white breast. Sexes similar. An all-white form lives only in Florida.

Great Blue Heron

The great blue heron might be the largest bird you're going to see without traveling too far from towns and cities. It lives exclusively near water—either fresh or salt—but the water might be no more than a drainage ditch, bayou, or marshy field. You'll recognize the heron most easily by its size: An adult gets up to 4 feet tall. When it flies, its neck curves into a graceful S, its wings beat slowly in a very dignified manner, and its legs hang down in an unusual unretracted mode.

On the ground, the heron stands on long legs and stalks haughtily through shallow water, its eyes trained downward, looking for fish, frogs, crawfish, and snakes. It may use its long yellow bill as a spear, stabbing with it more quickly than the eye can follow.

The heron nests high above the ground, building a large platform lined with fine twigs and green leaves. Often, herons will form a colony, and one tree may contain three or four nests.

Appearance:
13". Blue-gray above, white below, with a ragged, bushy crest, white collar around neck, broad gray breastband. Female has an additional rusty band across the upper belly.

Belted Kingfisher

The kingfisher lives exclusively near freshwater, and you won't see one unless you're out by a stream, river, or lake. If you are, though, the kingfisher has a distinctive, greased-back and crested "hair-do" that makes it quite easy to recognize. In addition, the multi-talented kingfisher is a divebombing specialist, and you won't mistake his act very quickly. After jinking around over the water in a halting, zigzag flight pattern, the kingfisher will suddenly pause and then plunge, headfirst, coming up most of the time with a fish in its long, dagger-like bill.

For their nest, a kingfisher pair will dig a tunnel in a bank near their fishing ground, kicking out the dirt with their feet and using their bills as shovels. The tunnel ends in a little domed chamber where the female will lay six to seven glossy white eggs. Understandably, given all the work that it takes, kingfishers like to reuse their tunnel from one year to the next.

Kingfishers are good-sized birds, a little over a foot long as adults. Their cry is a raspy, loud rattle, and they're nonvegetarians, preferring to dine on small fish, tadpoles, salamanders, frogs, and insects.

In recent years, the kingfisher has become a less common water bird as streams and rivers have been dammed or diverted.

Red-Winged Blackbird

The red-winged blackbird is the ultimate "what-else-could-you-call-it" bird. It is glossy, jet black with bright red shoulder patches edged in yellow. It's a real confidence-builder for the beginning birder. There's no mistaking it.

When spring arrives, the males are first to appear, each one staking out his turf. Females arrive several weeks later, and the males greet them with frenzied "courtship displays": energetic, aerial chase scenes with red patches flashing. Pairs settle down in colonies, with males continuing to defend territory from the tops of reeds and fenceposts. Females tend to stay hidden in the vegetation.

Red-winged blackbirds live in pastures, marshes, irrigated fields, and along roadsides. Their nests are often near or over water, made out of grasses and other vegetation, and hung fairly low in reeds or bushes. Their diet is mostly seeds and insects.

Appearance: 7–9½". After courtship, male's red shoulder patches are often hidden, with only the yellow edge showing. Female is streaky brown, resembling a large sparrow but with a longer bill.

Field Guides

The Audubon Society Pocket Guides: *Familiar Birds of North America: Eastern Region; Western Region* (Chanticleer Press/Knopf).

The Audubon Society Field Guide to North American Birds: Eastern Region; Western Region (Knopf).

Birds of North America: A Guide to Field Identification (Golden Press).

The Peterson Field Guide Series: *A Field Guide to Birds' Nests; A Field Guide to the Birds of Eastern and Central North America; A Field Guide to Western Birds* (Houghton Mifflin).

Field Guide to the Birds of North America (National Geographic Society)

For More Information

Audubon Handbooks: *Eastern Birds; How to Identify Birds; Western Birds* (Chanticleer Press/McGraw-Hill).

Bird Behavior (Robert Burton; Knopf).

The Birder's Handbook: A Field Guide to the Natural History of North American Birds (Paul R. Ehrlich, David S. Dobkin, and Darryl Wheye; Simon and Schuster/Fireside Books).

Book of North American Birds (Reader's Digest).

Stokes Nature Guides: *A Guide to Bird Behavior*, Volumes I, II, III (Donald W. Stokes; Little, Brown).